Esther

FOR SUCH A TIME AS THIS

CWR

Lynn Penson

For list of National Distributors, visit www.cwr.org.uk/distributors

Unless otherwise indicated, all Scripture references are from the Holy Bible: New International Version (NIV), copyright © 1973, 1978, 1984 by the International Bible Society.
The Message: Scripture taken from *The Message*. Copyright © 1993, 1994, 1995, 1996, 2000, 2001, 2002. Used by permission of NavPress Publishing Group.

Concept development, editing, design and production by CWR
Cover image: iStockphoto/Shawnz

Printed in the UK by Linney

ISBN: 978-1-85345-511-7

Contents

Introduction

Towards the end of 2008, at a meeting of my small group, we began the evening by sharing something of what was going on in our lives at that time. When it came to me, the responsibility of writing a Bible study guide on Esther – something I was just about to embark on – was my chief concern. Our group leader suggested we divert from his plan for the evening and simply read through this book from the Old Testament. This we did, stopping at the end of each chapter to mull over its contents together. It was an excellent evening, made all the more interesting by one young mum, not long a Christian, who had not heard of this character Esther; watching her, wide-eyed, as the story unfolded, was a great experience.

As a result of that evening, I was reminded of three things as I began my work.

Firstly, I was reminded of the incredible story that can be found in this book. I remember as a child being told an edited version of the story of Esther and, a little more recently, enjoying a Sunday series at my previous church. Like many people, I love a good story and within our Christian tradition we really do have some of the best. We have the story of Joseph, the musical of which is still playing to West End audiences as I write; we also have the stories of Daniel, Ruth, Hosea and Gomer to name just a few more in the Old Testament. The mastery Jesus displayed in telling His short but powerful stories, the accounts of Paul's journeys, and more recent stories of Gladys Aylward, Jim Elliot and George Müller, amongst others, have all enthralled and inspired me. As for this story of Esther, it is a piece of history that has it all – we have the ever-popular themes of good conquering evil, and rags to riches. We have tears and intense sorrow; we have great joy and celebration; both fasting and feasting play a major part in this drama. And what a line-up of characters! We have Haman, wicked beyond belief, rich, powerful and egotistical; a king who is out for a good time and happy to let others pick up responsibility; and Mordecai, determined and esteemed. We have the proud Vashti, imprudent Zeresh and then Esther, an orphaned girl from an ethnic minority who becomes the wealthiest and most powerful woman in the land. She is literally the star of the show; her name means star and in this woman we have a bright and shining star producing light in a dark world, bringing about the salvation of her people from annihilation.

Something else that I was reminded of was that we will all start from a different point of view so will see different things and come to different conclusions. I have read, lived and breathed this story for a little while, but each of you must come to it open to what God is saying to you. If you are doing this as a group study, give permission to each other to disagree amongst yourselves – and with me! Listen to and learn from each other. Bring your own story and personal perspective into the room so that you can enrich one another. If you are doing this as a personal study, spend time observing and listening to others to enhance your own thoughts.

The third thing that struck me has grown as I have been 'living with' Esther, and it relates to God's part in the narrative. The book of Esther is unique as a biblical book in that the name of God is not mentioned, nor is prayer or anything else that we might want to class as 'spiritual', except for fasting. Do you ever wonder where God is? Whether in national or international situations or closer to home in our difficult circumstances, we sometimes feel that God is absent. In the book of Esther it seems that God is hidden, yet He is present and active. This can give us courage and confidence that God is present and at work even when we are not aware of Him. There may be times when you pray and the problem is solved but the answer may have come in such a way that you do not see God's hand in it. You may have expected God to use your vicar, pastor or home group leader, but your help has come from a source that you least expected. Esther reminds us not to put God in a box, but to be aware of His presence in all of life's circumstances.

As you work through this study you will be encouraged to look at the characters and to reflect on who *you* are, maybe to set new goals, and to recognise that God is at work, even though we do not always recognise it, and that He can work through us even if we feel inadequate. I think of Paul writing, 'God chose the foolish things of the world to shame the wise' (1 Cor. 1:27).

And finally, be encouraged to celebrate with 'joy and feasting' (Esth. 9:19)!

UTLEY = YouTube

WEEK 1

Splendour and Glory

Opening Icebreaker

What is the most memorable celebration you have attended? Think about the experience using each of your senses; what you saw, smelled, tasted, heard and touched. What is it that makes it so memorable to you?

Bible Readings

Esther 1:1–2:1
Ephesians 5:21–33

Opening Our Eyes

I wonder what it was that made your celebration memorable. My guess is that no matter how good (or how bad) it was, it would not have attained to the scale of feasting we read about in the first chapter of Esther. This was partying the like of which would be hard to match.

For six months, the king wined and dined these leaders, princes and nobles, whilst displaying his great wealth. As if that was not enough, he ensured that everyone in Susa was included in the final seven days, and the wine flowed freely throughout. What a character!

The historian Herodotus informs us that the king appeared to be quite a contradictory character – sometimes impulsive and indecisive, whilst at other times bold, ambitious, visionary, and a confident leader. He was superstitious, and he was a womaniser. About Queen Vashti we know nothing other than what we read in this passage.

It would seem that everyone in the palace and beyond in Susa was having a good time – but then comes one of those moments when everything changes. It's a seemingly small but critical moment in history, with far-reaching consequences; the inebriated king sends for the queen. He has shown every piece of wealth and splendour that he possesses; it has all been displayed, discussed and admired and he is feeling rather pleased with himself. But after six months it is all somewhat passé. He needs something new to show off, something else to be congratulated on. What else could there possibly be? His wife! And so the eunuchs are dispatched with instructions to bring the queen wearing her royal crown. Some commentators have suggested that this instruction suggests that she should come wearing only her royal crown so that she could be admired in all her fleshly beauty. Whether or not this was the case we do not know, but it was certainly an inappropriate request. Women did not socialise with men, hence Vashti's separate banquet for the women. The intention to display her loveliness was not going to give Vashti a sense of being valued as a great beauty, but rather to fill her with fear and dread. It was unlikely that her appearance in a room of drunken men would have brought her dignified respect and admiration.

Vashti would have been very aware of the king's determination and his abhorrence of being thwarted. As a woman she had no rights in this relationship. What a quandary she was in!

She refuses to come, and then the quandary is the king's. After all the king's show of power and wealth, after all the fawning of those around him, the wife that he would have seen as his possession refuses his command! And so Xerxes consults with his 'experts'. I wonder what worried these experts most. Was it getting their answer right so that the king's fury didn't turn on them? Was it concern over how their own wives might react after hearing of this disobedience? The restoring and healing of relationships does not appear to be high on their agenda.

Memucan's verdict is delivered with hardness, clarity and authority. For the good of the kingdom, and to maintain the authority of men, Vashti must be replaced, never to enter the king's presence again. This is written in law that made it absolute and intractable.

And so the irreversible deed was done.

Discussion Starters

1. Slowly read Esther 1:4–8 and paint a picture in your mind. What word or phrase sums up your impression of this banquet?

   Extreme, Extravagance Lavish, Decadent, drunkenness.

2. What sort of a person is conjured up in your mind when you read of Xerxes? Which people do you read of, hear of, or know personally who might share some of these characteristics?

   Trump. Henry 8th

3. Imagine the entrance and announcement of the eunuchs into the banquet given by Vashti. Consider how the women and Vashti herself might think, feel and respond.

   Disgusted – Not taking it Seriously humiliation.

4. Can you think of a situation where you have been asked to do something that you disliked, found inappropriate or unacceptable? How did you react, and what were your feelings as you responded?

5. The king sought advice and was duly given it. What do you think about this advice? When you need advice, do you look to those who might say what you want to hear, or to those who might give good but challenging advice?

6. What issues are raised about the place of women in Persian society, and how does it compare with the twenty-first century? To what extent has the 'curse' recorded in Genesis 3:16 been true over history and to the present day?

7. How does the Christian picture of marriage presented by Paul in Ephesians 5:21–33 differ from the relationship between Xerxes and Vashti?

8. As you reflect on the various characters in this chapter, what do you a) admire and b) dislike in them? Can you see any of your own character traits reflected in these people? How does this challenge you?

Personal Application

Very early in the story we are introduced to distinctive personal and relational styles in the characters portrayed. We need to consider what can happen when we give instructions or advice, or make decisions, when we are not in the best frame of mind to do so. We should take care in seeking out sound and impartial advice.

As the scene unfolds, revealing the consequences of words and actions, we are prompted to consider that our actions and words have consequences both for ourselves and others. A good look at ourselves may reveal that we do not always act wisely. This might be a good time to ask the Holy Spirit to help us.

Seeing Jesus in the Scriptures

Vashti took a stand, knowing the consequences of such an action. We see in Jesus One who was not swayed by those around Him but stood for what was right, knowing the response of the religious leaders and the ultimate consequences.

What a contrast there is between Xerxes, who put on lavish displays of wealth to show his power and status, and Jesus, who was born, brought up and lived in humble surroundings; who had 'nowhere to lay his head' (Matt. 8:20). In His teaching we see that it is what is in a person's heart that is important, not status or wealth.

What a challenge! Following Jesus will not be the easy option, but we need to remain clear about what is of lasting and eternal value.

WEEK 2

Star!

Opening Icebreaker

What is a role model? Who are some of the 'heroes' in today's world? Are they good or bad examples? Who might see *you* as a role model? What do you feel you can bring to that relationship?

Bible Readings

Esther 2; 6:1–3
Proverbs 31:10–12,25–26
Luke 1:26–33
1 Peter 3:3–4
Matthew 11:29
Galatians 5:22–26

Opening Our Eyes

Vashti's fate is sealed; there is no going back on the king's decree, made known throughout the kingdom. I wonder how Xerxes felt – perhaps embarrassed, maybe ashamed and with regrets. I wonder if his attendants started to get worried. Maybe he was getting moody and bad-tempered. Of course, he may have been pleased not to have Vashti around any more but my instinct, as I read the opening of chapter 2, is that he had misgivings and was experiencing sadness at the loss of his queen. As we read chapter 2, we can see that he was in less buoyant mood than in chapter 1.

I can imagine Xerxes' servants getting together to share their anxieties and coming up with this scheme to avert trouble. And what a clever plan. We know from Herodotus that Xerxes was a womaniser; even his sister-in-law and daughter were not safe. What he needed was not just one woman but a whole harem of the most beautiful in the land – and why not make it into a competition? Not surprisingly, Xerxes' regrets over Vashti fade into the background at such a thought.

Can you imagine the scandal that such an occurrence would cause now? The country was scoured and hundreds of beautiful young women taken from their homes for months of preparation for a one-night stand with the king, only to be doomed to confinement in their harem quarters with no hope of marriage, love, children or freedom for the rest of their lives. All, that is, except for the one 'lucky winner'. It is thought that around 400 women were involved; a lot of women had to live as virtual widows, with many families losing a daughter and many young men losing their sweetheart.

I wonder what the atmosphere was like in the harem. No doubt a number were fearful and homesick, whilst others were prepared to do anything to attain the place of next

first lady. I am not a fan of 'reality' TV or competitions
to find the next star of the show, but the snippets I
have seen do not always show human nature in its best
and kindest form. No doubt there was considerable
backbiting, deceit, intrigue, bullying and unpleasantness
in this particular contest.

Amongst all of this was a young woman whose name was
probably derived from the Persian word for star, and she
really was going to be the star of the show. Her name?
Esther. Her Hebrew name, Hadassah, means myrtle;
myrtle branches are carried at the Feast of Tabernacles
and signify peace and thanksgiving.

So what do we know of Esther?

She was a young Jewish woman, one of an ethnic
minority whose ancestors had originally been brought
as exiles when Jerusalem was conquered. Having been
orphaned she was brought up by her cousin Mordecai
who treated her as his own daughter. And she sounds
rather stunning.

As this chapter unfolds we are introduced to a woman
who is not just beautiful to look at but also beautiful
inside. I am reminded of *The Message* version of Gabriel's
greeting to Mary in Luke 1:28: 'Good morning! You're
beautiful with God's beauty, Beautiful inside and out!
God be with you.'

We discover some very precious characteristics in Esther
as we read on.

Discussion Starters

1. Consider what you think life would have been like for Esther and the other women in the harem.

2. Why did Mordecai want Esther to keep her background a secret? What do you think about his insistence that Esther do so?

3. Read chapter 2:9–10,15,17,20,22. What picture of Esther do these verses portray?

4. What qualities in other people's characters do you most admire? Which of those qualities do you share?

5. When the plot to kill Xerxes was uncovered, Esther could have taken the credit for saving her husband's life. Think about situations known to you where credit has been attributed fairly – and times when it has not. What impact has this had on you, and others?

_____

_____

_____

_____

6. The incident of Mordecai's involvement in saving the king's life seems to have been overlooked, even forgotten. However, it was brought back to Xerxes' mind and was going to be of great significance later on. Have there been times when you could see no purpose in things that happened, yet later you saw their significance?

_____

_____

_____

_____

7. Think of one insight from this session that has particularly challenged you. Pray about it, share it or discuss it with others.

_____

_____

_____

_____

Personal Application

What a contrast between Esther and the characters we met in chapter 1! We have little insight into her life and only cameo shots of the sort of person she was. However, we see a young woman who seems to move with ease among those with whom she is compelled to live. She doesn't rebel or make a big show of herself. Though strikingly beautiful, it is not just her physical appearance that draws people to her. As we move about at work, at church, or in our communities, do we 'win the favour' of others or do we upset, frustrate or annoy them so that they are pleased to see us move on?

In Esther we meet a young woman who rose to the highest position in the land, yet did not turn her back on her surrogate father. What humility! How good are we at remembering those who have helped us to get where we are, whether it be parents, teachers, mentors or friends?

Maybe this is a good time to reflect on what we have learned from others and to commit to thanking them for what they have done for us.

Seeing Jesus in the Scriptures

I am reminded of words from 1 Peter 3:3–4 to wives: 'Your beauty should… be that of your inner self, the unfading beauty of a gentle and quiet spirit'. However, this is not only a characteristic to be admired in women, as Jesus refers to Himself as being 'gentle and humble in heart' (Matt. 11:29) and He is a role model above all others for both sexes.

WEEK 3

For Such a Time...

Opening Icebreaker

Look at some recent newspapers or think about what has been in the news in the wider media. If you were preparing to be a politician or local councillor, which contemporary issue would you want to take a stand on?

Bible Readings

Esther 3:1–4:14
Proverbs 29:11–12
1 Samuel 17:32–37

Opening Our Eyes

No sooner do we draw breath from the events of the previous chapters than we find the story racing on to yet another plot.

We found Mordecai sitting at the 'king's gate' back in Esther 2:21, and again here in chapter 3. This is meaningful because this particular location was the place of justice; the accused stood whilst the judge sat. This suggests that Mordecai worked in the king's service, or had gained promotion to it, perhaps through the influence of Esther. This is what gave him the opportunity to overhear the plot against the king's life and to gain access to the king's courts. It was also going to bring him to the attention of Haman.

Enter Haman! And what an entrance he makes, with the royal officials kneeling down to him as he makes his way through the king's gate. That is, all the officials bar one – Mordecai. We are not told why Mordecai refused but later events give us good reason to deduce the reasons. No doubt Haman's cruel and deceitful character was evident even at this stage.

Mordecai's lack of respect might have gone unnoticed but for the other officials. Were they annoyed on behalf of Haman or riled by the fact that they were bowing down yet this Jewish man was not? Once brought to his attention, Haman's fury increased when he discovered that Mordecai was a Jew.

A contributing factor to the feud that developed was probably that Haman was an Agagite. The Agagites had a grudge against the Jews going back to an incident where Samuel put King Agag to death after Saul's disobedience in sparing his life (see 1 Sam. 15:33). Prejudice which is passed on throughout generations resulting in bitterness and malice continues to be evident in our own day. Haman's hatred and desire for revenge is out of all proportion and reflects how evil magnifies as it takes root. The first thing he does is to seek guidance by casting lots, to know when it would be best to carry out his intended massacre. The fact that he has to wait for a year is quite acceptable, but he wants it confirmed in legislation immediately so that it cannot be revoked.

His conversation with the king shows the extent of his deceit and manipulation. It also shows that Xerxes has not learned his lesson of being wary of his advisors. He does not enquire further of Haman, and is prepared to accept the information that has been fed to him without any verification. The die is cast and the people of Susa and beyond are stunned at the news that this minority ethnic group, who had lived alongside the Persians for many years, is to face wholesale slaughter.

Esther, shut away in the palace, has no idea what is going on, but is distraught to hear of Mordecai's distress. Mordecai ensures that Esther is provided with accurate and full information as he appeals for her intervention. Esther is understandably reluctant, knowing the risk to her life of going to the king without his summons. But Mordecai leaves her in no doubt of her duty and her own peril whether she goes to the king or not.

In Mordecai's statement that if Esther does not help, salvation for the Jews would come from elsewhere (Esth. 4:14), we have the one veiled insight into Mordecai's belief that such help would come from God who would not allow His people to be annihilated.

Discussion Starters

1. Consider the possible reasons why Mordecai refused to bow down to Haman. He did not know that the consequence of this refusal was to put his people in danger, but do you think he was right to take this stand?

_____

_____

2. Think of people who have put their own or other people's freedom (or even lives) at risk by taking a stand on a matter of importance. What is your opinion of this action?

_____

_____

3. Dianne Tidball writes 'how frequently we are reluctant to go even so far as risking embarrassment in order to question what is not right'.[1] Do you think this is true? Explore your response to this statement.

_____

_____

4. Have there been times when you have a) taken or b) avoided taking such a risk? How did you feel? What were the consequences?

_____

_____

5. Make a note of the processes employed by Haman in getting his plan actioned. What does this tell us about him? Are there characters like Haman around today?

_____

_____

6. Mordecai and the Jews responded with great mourning. What did this involve? How do we respond to grief? What would you consider to be a healthy and appropriate way of mourning?

_____

_____

7. It was to be a year before the annihilation of the Jews was to take place. What effect do you think this would have on the Jews and on the people who lived alongside them?

_____

_____

8. Consider the flaws in both Haman and Xerxes as leaders. What qualities should we look for in our leaders?

_____

_____

9. What do you think of Mordecai's response to Esther's fear of going to the king?

_____

_____

Personal Application

Haman's response to Mordecai was vicious and
unrestrained. He seemed not only to be angered by the
denial of respect but also influenced by racial motives.
His prejudice would have been handed down from
his forefathers. Prejudice is something we may deny in
ourselves but if we dig deeper we may feel uncomfortable
with what we find. We are not going to attempt Haman's
type of revenge but we may find ourselves reacting
negatively about somebody without due cause. Equally,
like Xerxes, we may be ready to believe what we hear
without thinking carefully and checking it out.

These are issues we need to consider and apply to our
own thinking and behaviour.

Seeing Jesus in the Scriptures

Jesus was a wonderful role model for accepting people
as they were and for treating them with grace whilst
challenging their lifestyles. I think of the woman who
had been caught in the act of adultery and was brought
to Him (John 8:1–11). He was not going to assign her to
the fate suggested by her accusers, nor was He going to
fall into their trap to trip Him up. Rather, He challenged
the accusers themselves. That is just one example of the
way Jesus related to people. We see in Jesus someone
who treated each person with dignity, impartiality and
consideration – very different from both Haman and Xerxes.

We also see in Him One who did not hold back from
treading a dangerous path, One who was not just going
to bring salvation to exiled Jews, but to all who are
prepared to follow Him.

[1]Dianne Tidball, *Esther A True First Lady* (Ross-shire: Christian Focus
Publications, 2001) p63.

2 weeks -
20-6-17

WEEK 4

Waiting, Fasting, Stillness

Opening Icebreaker

Listen to some quiet and reflective music. Follow this with a period of silence. Decide beforehand how long this time will be; I suggest four to five minutes. Then, think about how you found the time of silence. Was it welcomed, or uncomfortable for you? Share with others anything that comes to mind.

Bible Readings

Esther 4:15–5:8
Psalm 27:14
Isaiah 30:15
Exodus 34:28
2 Samuel 12:16–17
1 Kings 21:27
Ezra 8:21,23

Opening Our Eyes

Up to now we have looked at the 'big picture' through the narrative of events as they unfold in the book of Esther. For this study we are going to take a small part of the story, put it under the microscope and use it as a launch pad to look into the themes of waiting, fasting and stillness.

We ended our last study with Mordecai's challenge to Esther ringing in our ears. The queen was left in no doubt about her cousin's wishes; he told her that she was to risk her life to plead for the Jews, and if she did not, she would face death herself even though the Jewish people as a whole would be saved in some other way. It might seem that there was no real choice, but maybe she believed that if she kept quiet and thought hard she would find a way out in the intervening twelve months.

What a remarkable change takes place as Esther moves from following instructions from her cousin to taking a clear and decisive role. She is now giving Mordecai instructions with clarity and authority as she calls for all the Jews in Susa to join herself and her maids for a full three-day total fast.

No mention is made of God, nor is there a specific reference to prayer, though it is included in the apocryphal version where both Mordecai and Esther plead with God.

It is clear that something very profound is taking place, something that will be of great value to us if we listen to, and learn from, Esther. Esther has made the decision that she must approach the king, but rather than rushing in before 'losing her nerve', she waits. This is not procrastination, it is not an attempt to 'put off the evil hour', but is an intentional wait.

In pondering this it seems that a number of things are happening. Firstly, Esther is recognising her own inability to sort this out for herself. Her beauty and charm are not enough to get through this difficulty, and Mordecai cannot sort it out. In recognising her powerlessness she is admitting human weakness and the need for the all-powerful God to come alongside her and give her wisdom and success.

As I look back on my life, I see times when trouble came and I just waded in to try to sort it out; I did not always fail, but at times I certainly did not help. It took me a long time to even recognise this principle of admitting my own weakness and inability as being the first step to looking to God Himself. I have often needed to be both challenged and encouraged to remember that God's strength can be found in my weakness (2 Cor. 12:9).

One of my father's favourite sayings was 'Fools rush in where angels fear to tread' or, 'Act in haste, repent at leisure'. How many times do things get worse as a result of impulsive reactions or hastily made decisions? I have had to learn the hard way that emailing immediate responses can sometimes get me into deep waters. (Actually, I am still learning that lesson!) As we stop and wait we are better able take stock, think more objectively and get a better perspective.

Discussion Starters

1. Look again at Esther 4:12–14, and then on into verses 15–17. Discuss the emotions going on for both Esther and Mordecai. What new insights about Esther's character do we discover in these verses?

2. It seems that time was suspended for three days for fasting. Have you ever a) made a conscious decision to stop and wait for God's timing when something important was on your mind? b) rushed into a decision or action when you would have been better to wait? Reflect on both ways of responding.

3. Look at the following pre-Esther Old Testament references to fasting, and discuss what they suggest about this discipline: Exodus 34:28; 2 Samuel 12:16–17; 1 Kings 21:27; Ezra 8:21,23. Do you think that fasting is a way to get God to change His mind, or does it have some other purpose?

4. What is the significance of Esther's instruction to gather the entire Jewish population together to fast?

5. Fasting was assumed and practised by the early Christians. Do you think it still has a place today? Have you ever fasted? If not, would you consider it? What might prevent you or others from using this spiritual tool?

6. Fasting is usually associated with going without food for a period of time. What other forms of fasting may help to achieve the same results?

7. Read Esther 5:1–8 slowly. Picture the scene, feel the atmosphere and emotion. What strikes you personally from this event?

8. Even after three days of fasting Esther was in no hurry to do business with Xerxes. Why do you think that might be?

9. Reflect on one aspect of this study that has
a) encouraged you b) challenged you.

Personal Application

This study poses the question, 'Where do you go and
what do you do when trouble lands at your door?' Esther
shows how it is possible to put aside our own fears and
find out what God wants us to do – and then do it in His
timing. It may be that further exploration of the spiritual
disciplines of fasting, prayer, solitude and silence may
help you in finding direction and spiritual maturity.

We see the strength that can be found in solidarity as
well as in solitude, joining with others to seek for God's
will. I take great comfort in seeing how God could take a
humble Jewish girl, elevate her to the position of queen
and, more importantly, enable her to save her people.
How wonderful to remember that we are sons and
daughters of the King of kings, and that God can use us
no matter how inadequate we may feel. We can take our
courage and confidence from our Father God.

Seeing Jesus in the Scriptures

Jesus fasted before He started His earthly ministry (Matt.
4:2) and He assumed His followers fasted too (see Matt.
6:16–18; Mark 2:18), although He did not insist on it. He
also regularly took time out to be with His Father despite
the many demands on Him, and especially when He was
preparing for an important event or decision. We see in
His life this discipline of stopping and waiting to hear
from God. If it was important for Him, how much more
important is it for us?

WEEK 5

Anger and Pride

Opening Icebreaker

Think about recent news stories which include incidents of anger, rage, bitterness, greed and cruelty. How might these stories have turned out if the situations had been handled with calmness and peace?

Bible Readings

Esther 5:7–7:10
Romans 12:9–21
Ephesians 4:26–27,31
Philippians 2:1–11
1 Peter 5:5

Opening Our Eyes

The narrative reaches breathtaking proportions in this study. It is difficult to list the many adjectives that could be used to describe the events as they now unfold.

In the last session, we read of Esther's first banquet for the king and Haman. Why didn't she make her request then? She had been promised anything she desired, up to half of Xerxes' kingdom. How could she delay? Yet delay she does! She has not spent three days in total fasting to rush in now. We might be tempted to believe she got cold feet; but I think it far more likely that she had a sense that this was not the right time.

Esther 5:9–14 gives such insight into Haman's character. Can you see him? Proud and haughty yet animated, grinning from ear to ear and with a definite bounce in his step as he leaves the palace with the invitation of the queen ringing in his ears. How quickly his joy turns to anger as he passes Mordecai, who would now have changed from his clothes of mourning to resume his place at the king's gate. What timing!

Back home, Haman wants to share his excitement and self-importance, though his bitterness towards Mordecai soon spills over. The plan for the gallows to be built is hatched and we see how easily swayed Haman is by his friends and family. He has risen to such a high rank, yet has not learned the lesson of weighing up advice and taking its source into consideration.

He wastes no time in getting the gallows built; he must have had his men working through the night to get the job finished by first thing in the morning. This is no ordinary gallows. At seventy-five feet (or twenty-three metres) high, neither the gallows nor the demise of the person it is intended for is going to be missed. It has been suggested that its height has been exaggerated, a figure plucked to signify its enormity; whether this is the case or not, the intention was that no one was going to miss finding out what happens when you mess with Haman.

With that all done, he is off to put his request to the king. There he is met with a surprise. The king wants advice on how best to honour someone special. Haman's delight and arrogance know no bounds as he replies. Isn't it extraordinary how we can leap to conclusions? Some of us might find we immediately leap to *negative* conclusions, thinking that people believe the worst in us. The arrogant Haman's response shows the reverse, and we read what he desires for himself; he wants the entire population to recognise his power and status as nearly equal to that of the king himself. What an ego! And what a shock to then discover this pomp and ceremony is for his arch-enemy. To make it even more humiliating, he is to be the one to orchestrate it!

The shame is too much to bear as he rushes home, crushed and horrified, to relate the incident to his family and friends. And what a group of 'Job's comforters' they are. It is interesting to read of their prediction of Haman's ruin due to Mordecai's Jewish origins, even though Haman has referred to this in his previous conversation (Esth. 5:13).

Could the day get any worse? It could and it would!

Discussion Starters

1. List and explore the effects of Haman's character seen in this session, and remember some of the points made in week 3.

2. Haman was eaten up by his anger and resentment. To what extent do we see these negative feelings in our society? Have you ever recognised them in yourself? In what situations are you most likely to experience these emotions?

3. How can we avoid such attitudes? Think about coping structures and devices you have employed and which might be helpful to share with others.

4. What contrasts do you see between the characters of Esther and Zeresh?

5. The king had a sleepless night. Can you think of other times when biblical characters have had disturbed or dream-filled nights? What might this indicate about the way in which God works in people?

6. Why do you think Mordecai's Jewishness was of concern to Haman's advisors?

7. Esther now openly identified with her Jewish fellow countrymen. Why is the timing of her revelation so crucial?

8. Read again Esther's response to the king's question as to what she wanted. What attitudes and skills did she display?

9. What is your response to Xerxes' condemnation of Haman?

Personal Application

In this section we see human nature at its worst and ugliest with evidence of hatred, anger, bitterness, malice, revenge, cruelty, arrogance and pride. Although not carried to such extremes, there is probably something of these traits in all of us. For example, how many of us recognise pride in ourselves? We look at others, and believe ourselves to be a better manager, solicitor, engineer, shop assistant, or teacher; and how do we feel about having a smarter car, bigger house, more money, cleaner home, or children who excel in sport, music or academically? Taking pride in our work and giving our best is commendable but doing it in such a way that other people feel put down is not. This may be a good time to reflect on what we can do to avoid or tackle negative thinking, behaviour and emotions.

Seeing Jesus in the Scriptures

In Jesus we see the antidote to the ugliness of Haman; a Man whose emotions were healthy. He felt anger in the right way, for the right things at the right time. He was angry at injustice, hypocrisy, and lack of compassion (Mark 3:5; John 2:13–17). However, He also warned against being angry without good cause (Matt. 5:22) and taught that we need to maintain good relationships by sorting out difficulties with each other (Matt. 5:23–24).

The humility of Jesus, seen in Philippians 2:5–11, contrasts vividly with what we have been reading.

WEEK 6

Consequences

Opening Icebreaker

Think about an action-adventure movie that has proved popular. Why do you think such films, often featuring fictional murder and violence, are regarded as entertaining?

Bible Readings

Esther 8:1–9:17
Romans 12:1–2,17–21
Proverbs 21:1–2
Ephesians 2:14

Opening Our Eyes

Those of us of a certain age will almost certainly remember Margaret Thatcher's words, 'The lady's not for turning'. Well, here is a king who did such a huge and rapid turnaround it almost makes you feel dizzy.

We know from the historian Herodotus that the property of a condemned criminal automatically reverted back to the estates of the king. Rather than keeping it to add to his personal wealth, Xerxes gives Haman's very substantial estate to Queen Esther, making her a very wealthy woman in her own right. Esther now discloses the fact that she is related to Mordecai, who is elevated to the highest position in the land on receiving the king's ring, which has been reclaimed from Haman. Mordecai is described in Esther 8:15 as wearing royal garments, a gold crown and purple robe, probably as he had done the day he was paraded by Haman through the streets – but this time it is not just for a few hours. This is further evidence of his great status.

At this point, Esther's life is secure and it seems that she has all she could want, including the knowledge that Mordecai is also secure. The first part of her request made in Esther 7:3 has been granted; her life has been spared. However, it appears that in the turmoil the king has lost sight of the second part of her request – to spare the lives of her people. And so she identifies with them, pleading for their salvation. Notice how she approaches Xerxes. Despite the great change in her personal circumstances she continues to be respectful, even hesitant; she is also very careful not to implicate her husband in Haman's plot, even though he was ultimately responsible for the edict.

Once a decree had been issued in the king's name it could not be revoked, so Xerxes could not change the orders sent by Haman. Instead, another decree had to go out that would preclude the first one being carried through. It is interesting to note the king's response. Esther is saved, and that is his prime concern. He then gives authority to Esther and Mordecai to sort out the rest. Despite having been caught out before by not taking responsibility, he is doing it again. Mordecai has the orders written and sent throughout the Persian provinces with great haste.

What we read here is not quite the 'they all lived happily ever after' ending we might have liked to round off this remarkable drama. Here is a rags-to-riches account of an orphan girl marrying a rich and important man; a story in which we also have the picture of arrogance and evil being overcome by good. The decision to hang Haman was Xerxes' judgment, so is beyond the influence of our hero and heroine. Indeed for Haman to be, as it were, hoisted by his own petard, highlights justice being done. So far so good. However, what comes next is perhaps more difficult for us, as 21st-century Christians to understand. Our belief in compassion and kindness, even towards our enemies, seems at variance with what we read of the widespread slaying of the enemies of the Jews. But what this shows is that Esther and Mordecai ensure their job is completed; any weakness at this stage would have cost the Jewish people dearly.

Discussion Starters

1. Esther made no assumptions in her request despite all that had happened. Look at the way she pleaded with Xerxes. Is there anything we can learn from her way of negotiating?

2. We have a moving scene of Esther tearfully pleading for the lives of her people. Consider the things that are a great burden to you. They may be personal, global or spiritual matters. It would be good to pray about these things rather than just discussing them.

3. What is your immediate/instinctive reaction to the edict as recorded in Esther 8:11–12? Why do you think this edict was necessary?

4. What was the response of the Jews to this edict? And what was the response of the other nations? What do you think of this?

5. Look at the effect of this edict, described in Esther 9:1–17. What do you believe is the relevance of the comment, repeated twice, that hands were not laid on the plunder?

----

6. What do you think are the reasons for Esther's further request, recorded in Esther 9:13? Why would this be necessary?

----

7. What is your response to Esther 8:13, where we read that the Jews were ready to 'avenge themselves on their enemies'? What might be seen as a Christian attitude towards this avenging principle?

----

8. Think about areas of the world that are suffering atrocities today. What would your prayer be for them? Spend some time praying for these situations.

Personal Application

As the story of Esther unfolds we see the full extent of the horrors resulting from the chain of events leading back to Haman's first encounter with Mordecai. In the light of all that followed, was Mordecai right to take the stance he did in refusing to give honour to Haman? Would he have maintained it, had he known the consequences? There are times we need to take a stand, but we also need to think about the consequences, not just for ourselves but also in regard to the implications for others.

Seeing Jesus in the Scriptures

We see in the teaching of Jesus a way of living that stands in sharp contrast to a worldly view. He spoke about going the extra mile, loving and praying for your enemy, and not returning evil for evil (see Matt. 5:38–48). That is not to say that we allow situations like the one we read about in Esther, or the ones happening around the world today, to simply continue. However, we are challenged to behave in a way that is compassionate and kind.

In our own small world, do we want to exact revenge when someone has hurt us? Or do we live lives where our thinking and behaviour is transformed rather than conformed to what is often the world's standard?

APOCRYPH 1

WEEK 7

Celebrate with Joy!

Opening Icebreaker

Think about the good things you have experienced over the last week, month or year. Write your own psalm of praise. One way of doing this is as an acrostic psalm where you write the words 'Thank you' or 'Praise' down the paper, and then use each letter as the first of a phrase or word that expresses your thanks.

Bible Readings

Esther 9:18–10:3
1 Samuel 7:12
Luke 22:19

 **Opening Our Eyes**

Some years ago my hairdresser invited my family to join
him in the celebration of Purim at his synagogue. What
an experience. The first part of the proceedings was a
formal service in Hebrew. Our youngest son, David, was
not overly impressed with needing to stay still in these
unfamiliar surroundings; nor was he keen on keeping
on his Kippah, the traditional skullcap worn by the men.
However, as the formal part of the proceedings came to
a close the whole atmosphere changed. We remained
in the main worship area as we moved seamlessly from
a solemn service into party mode. The story of Esther
was re-enacted. Cheers went up any time Esther and
Mordecai's names were read out whilst jeers, boos and
the stamping of feet greeted any mention of Haman's
name. Instruments and shakers were used to add to the
general mayhem. David's eyes grew wider and, after his
initial bafflement, he started to get into the swing and
enjoyed the fun. The entertainment included humorous
sketches where people dressed up and threw themselves
into the festivities. All this was followed by an excellent
buffet. David decided he liked the synagogue and was
a little disappointed that we would not be going there
regularly instead of going to our church!

Purim is the festival instituted by Mordecai and Esther
all those centuries ago as a way of remembering and
celebrating the events we have been exploring in this
series of Bible studies. Their immediate response of
feasting, celebration and present giving continues to
be commemorated annually.

Two things stand out to me here. One is the exuberant
and instinctive celebration; the other is the importance of
remembering. These are two features that are intrinsic to
Jewish culture.

In the Old Testament we read of God remembering people such as Noah, Abraham, Rachel and Hannah. He also remembers His love, His covenant to be gracious. He commands His people to remember Him and what He has done in setting them free from slavery in Egypt, and in keeping them safe in their wilderness wanderings. This is remembered every year in the special Passover meal.

In 1 Samuel 7:12 we read of Samuel setting up a memorial stone after a defeat of the Philistines. Its purpose was to act as a memorial to remember the help received from God. This engenders thankfulness and encourages trust in God who, having assisted on that occasion, is able to do so again.

We see this recurring pattern of remembering God's help and faithfulness throughout the Old Testament. At times this is marked by physical memorials; at other times, by celebrations. I love Michele Guinness' book, *The Heavenly Party*. Having come to Christian faith from a Jewish background where she enjoyed the joy, colour and food of the regular cycle of Jewish festivities she realised how much the Church had lost out on by not having such wholehearted celebrations. She writes, 'I don't know whose idea it was to make Western Christianity so lifeless and dull, but it certainly didn't come from God.'[1]

Purim was instituted to remember that God had not forgotten the Jewish people, and to celebrate His saving activity on their behalf. We as Christians also have much to celebrate.

Discussion Starters

1. Read through Esther 9:17–23,27–28. What are the instructions given about celebrating Purim?

2. Do you agree with Michelle Guinness' quotation that Western Christianity can be 'lifeless and dull'? If so, should it change? And how?

3. What do we learn a) about the character of Mordecai (see 10:2–3) and b) from the character of Xerxes?

4. What sorts of thing would you include in an obituary to Haman? Are there any 'Haman's' in your life? How might you respond to them in the light of New Testament teaching?

5. What one thing has challenged you about a) the character and b) the actions of Esther? What does this contribute to our understanding of her?

6. What do you understand to be the theological issues behind this story, where God is not mentioned? What have you learned about God and His care for His people in Exile through the book of Esther?

7. What parallels are there between Purim and the Eucharist (or Holy Communion)? Can we learn anything from the Jewish tradition as we remember the Last Supper?

8. How have you experienced God's care in your life in the past week, month, year?

Personal Application

The Jewish people in the Persian Empire wasted no time in celebrating their salvation. Not only was it to be celebrated then, but for generation after generation.

We have so much to be thankful for as we see God's saving work in our lives. How easy it is to take it all for granted, to become too comfortable with our faith, too familiar with Jesus, His life and His death on our behalf. We refer to 'celebrating' Communion or the Eucharist, but is this a good description? Whether you are studying this as a group or as an individual might I suggest you 'thought-shower' the things you have to be thankful for. Then consider how you could celebrate one or more of them with a group of friends. Go on! Enjoy yourself as you reflect on God's goodness in your life!

Seeing Jesus in the Scriptures

There seem to be three particular pointers as we look to Jesus from this section.

- Esther put her life on the line in order to save her people. Jesus laid down His life for our salvation.
- Jesus recognised the value of remembering and exhorted His followers to remember Him when they ate and drank (Luke 22:19).
- Jesus enjoyed a party; He even provided the best wine to ensure the party went well (John 2:1–11)!

It is worth spending some time considering these aspects of Jesus' life and work.

[1]Michele Guinness, *The Heavenly Party* (Oxford: Monarch Books, 2007) p18.

Leader's Notes

Week 1: Splendour and Glory

Icebreaker

The purpose of this is simply to get your group chatting and warming up to the idea of what is involved in a party in preparation for the description of Xerxes' feasting.

Aim of the Session

The first chapter of Esther is headed 'Queen Vashti Deposed' in the NIV, but this whole piece (and into chapter 2) interweaves aspects of the characters of the king, the queen and Memucan.

I have used the Greek form of the king's name – Xerxes – but some translations use the Persian form, Ahasuerus. He reigned from 486–465 BC. During the century in which he reigned, the historian Herodotus wrote *The Histories*. Whilst he does not include details of Esther, he does give us insight into the culture of the times, and into the character of Xerxes.

As we look at Xerxes we are introduced to a powerful man, publicly defied and humiliated by his queen, and who, by the end of the first chapter, was trying to hold on to his stately position. Joyce Baldwin writes about this great lawmaker, 'attempting to maintain his dignity'. He was a man 'whose law could not be altered' yet who was 'prepared to pass an edict in a moment of pique, when he was not even sober' and was advised by counsellors who were 'clever but hardly wise'.[1] What does this say about such power, in contrast to the all-powerful nature of God? In looking at the behaviour of Xerxes, we see a distinction between how the world judges success and power, and how God views it.

In Memucan's advice we see his fear of the loss of control the men may experience should their wives hear of Vashti's defiance, which is an insight into gender roles at the time. He believed that submission can be brought about by legislation. Yet godly submission is always in response to good authority and incorporates mutuality (Eph. 5:21). Sadly the king was carried along by Memucan's opinion rather than taking time to think and to consider his wife's part. The passage from Ephesians 5 reminds us of a Christian model of marriage which stands in sharp contrast to the relationship between the king and Vashti.

In Vashti, we see the character of a woman who had no rights, yet who was prepared to stand up to the inappropriate demand of the most powerful man in the land. Perhaps she recognised the disgrace his instruction would bring, not only to herself but also to him, when he was sober enough to remember. Her principled stand had consequences; she was to forfeit her crown, her role, her status and her relationship with the king.

Discussion Starter 6 may raise issues of submission that go beyond the context of this study. As leader you will need to consider whether this is a topic which is best returned to at a later stage with good preparation. However, the quote from Genesis is there to encourage the thought that man inappropriately 'ruling' over women is itself a curse to be freed from and not part of God's original order.

God has set standards for human relationships and behaviour, not in order to deprive us of freedom and fun but to ensure that we are able to enjoy living without harming ourselves and others. The last Discussion Starter gives an opportunity for personal reflection about what it means to live a godly life.

Week 2: Star!

Icebreaker

By looking at some of today's heroes and role models, you will be able to think about some of the positive and negative characteristics in people of influence. These will be indicators of what we admire in others in the twenty-first century. Much of this study is about reflecting on character and personality.

Aim of the Session

Whilst looking at character we must not get away from the fact that primarily this is a great story. It is good to get into the mood of the narrative and not to try to cover up the parts we may think are somewhat racy! The first Discussion Starter, about life in the harem, will help to root the account in the real-life situation of Esther. The Church can tend to be prudish at times, yet that certainly does not come from Scripture, which deals with life as it is.

It seems that self-centredness is rife in our society. And it is not just those 'out there'; how many of us can genuinely say that we never find ourselves living in this way? Whilst there is a great deal of kindness and generosity around, the 'dog eat dog' mentality is also very evident. People who want to get to the top will often climb over everyone and anyone in order to get there. It is tough for people of honesty and integrity to survive in the world of work, and that needs to be acknowledged and understood. However, the challenge is that we make a choice; we do not have to follow the world's standards. We can, in our own way, make a difference. It may not appear that this is so, but we do not possess the big picture. Little did Mordecai and Esther know the repercussions when Mordecai uncovered and passed on the assassination plot to Esther, and when

Esther passed on that knowledge to the king, attributing it to Mordecai. What we see, even though not voiced, is that God is at work even if He may appear absent or hidden. Whilst references from Proverbs about women have been included as suggested Bible readings, it is important that we recognise that qualities such as kindness, generosity and gentleness reach beyond gender boundaries. Note what is said in 'Seeing Jesus in the Scriptures', along with the reference from Galatians. For some of us the gentler qualities will come more naturally, whilst for others it is less easy. Our natural differences need to be recognised and valued, but these qualities are to be admired and encouraged. Later on, we see a certain ruthlessness in Esther so we must recognise that we are only dealing with a little of who she is at this point.

Note: Questions have been raised about the historicity of Queen Esther as she is not mentioned by the historian Herodotus or elsewhere. It has been suggested that Esther was a secondary wife, which is quite in keeping with both the biblical account and with the culture of the day.

Week 3: For Such a Time...

Icebreaker
This is designed to stimulate thought about taking a stand on difficult issues. If you are leading a group, you might find it useful to prepare some appropriate newspaper cuttings in advance.

Aim of the Session
In looking at Discussion Starter 1, the following might be helpful. Some would say that Mordecai refused to bow down to Haman because to do so was seen as idolatrous – as worshipping other gods – and so forbidden by the Torah. This could be considered as a good reason,

though bowing as a mark of respect is recorded in the Old Testament, particularly in respect to a king. It may have been linked with Haman being an Agagite, a tribe of the Amalekites. There was a long history of animosity between the Amalekites and the people of Israel – see Exodus 17:8–10 and 1 Samuel 15, especially verses 30–33.

There are numerous people in history who have suffered, died or faced possible death through the stand they have taken. We may think of some of the moving stories of the Early Church martyrs, followed by many more throughout history who have stood for the freedom to follow Christ. Tyndale was hounded to his death because of his determination to get the Bible translated into English; Martin Luther survived despite his most audacious stand against the authorities; and others such as Martin Luther King and Archbishop Romero have lost their lives speaking out against injustice. A number of African bishops have been killed in recent years, having made a political stand for justice. Such bravery extends to all parts of society. Many of us will remember the massacre of Chinese students at Tiananmen Square, and recall countless other such incidents. The familiar story of David's courage in facing Goliath is one of courage when facing an enemy (1 Sam. 17:32–37 – especially v37).

In discussing questions 3 and 4, it is essential to listen to each other with consideration and without passing judgments, so that people feel safe to share in an honest and secure environment.

In the reaction of Mordecai and his fellow Jews, we observe a very public display of grief. Even today we see a great contrast between the often solemn and dignified way death is treated in British culture, and that of the Middle East, where there is great wailing and displays of emotion. The aftermath of the death of the Princess of Wales showed a more open display of feeling, but even then the crowds were hushed as the funeral cortège proceeded. Exploring these different ways of grieving might be helpful to those who struggle with mourning loss of any kind. For these Jews, there was to be a year before annihilation. That would be significant. Under the Nazis, ways of discriminating against Jews came in gradually; the wearing of the yellow star to mark them out, the curfew, the restrictions on where they might go, the boycotting of shops and businesses; all these were to differentiate and humiliate them. The sense of loss for these Jews living in Persia would start the moment the decree was made public, as acts of discrimination crept in along with the loss of their hopes and dreams and future.

This horror came about through a combination of Haman's cruel hatred and Xerxes' lack of interest. Haman displayed such vindictiveness and prejudice, allowing his emotions to run away with him. We often hear of people in power being forced out of their jobs as a result of small errors, or as a result of bad judgments made by others. Sometimes it seems harsh that they appear to be the scapegoat. However, they are seen as culpable if they have allowed things to occur that they had the authority and opportunity to prevent. As we read in the well-known quote by Edmund Burke (1729–1797), 'The only thing necessary for the triumph of evil is for good men to do nothing'.

Week 4: Waiting, Fasting, Stillness

Icebreaker
The quiet music at the start of the session will help foster an atmosphere of stillness and calm. If you are leading a group, choose some reflective music and perhaps have it playing in the background as the others arrive.

Aim of the Session

It is easy to read this story superficially without recognising the full impact it would have had on the Jewish readers for whom it was originally intended.

Here we have a defining moment both for Queen Esther and for the Jewish nation. So much rests on Esther, and yet ultimately God will determine the outcome. We witness the transformation of a young woman ready to please all and obey her father-figure into a woman of dignity, maturity, clear thinking and amazing wisdom. Her first decision was truly great.

It has been pointed out that fasting was a sign of Esther's own sense of weakness and need of God's strength. Fasting is often a sidelined topic today but this is a good opportunity to tackle it, and you may find that you or your group would like to have a better understanding of what it is about. I recommend *Celebration of Discipline* by Richard Foster[2], which devotes a chapter to this subject along with other pertinent topics. Foster points out that fasting must firstly centre on God but that it achieves other things too. It reveals the things that control us, reminds us that we are nourished and sustained by God, helps keep balance in our lives by helping us find our priorities, and may also give guidance in decisions and increase effectiveness in our prayer life. Foster suggests applying fasting to contemporary culture. This may include fasting from people, TV, social media, games consoles, clothes shopping, or from other aspects of our consumer culture. Have some fun exploring your responses to Discussion Starter 5.

Fasting is part of the discipline of waiting for God's guidance rather than rushing in with our own agenda and solutions. This is not a passive waiting; a time to put our feet up and wait for God to come and sort it all out.

Rather, it is an active waiting where we choose to listen to God, to allow Him to bring about the solution in His way and His time. This is a vital lesson to learn from the study on Esther.

The Jews had already been fasting (Esth. 4:3) but what Esther wanted was coordinated community fasting. For Esther, fasting was to be a corporate, not just an individual activity. She recognised that she needed the support of others alongside her. How many of us, when in trouble, not only neglect going to God but are also too proud to recognise that we need support from our fellow Christians? God made us firstly to relate to Him, but also for relationship with others. There is something special and powerful when a church or a group of Christians stand together to fight injustice or evil, or when they stand with each other for support through difficult times. This is why the pictures of being part of a body or a building are used by Paul in the New Testament, and why we are urged to meet together, to encourage and 'spur one another on' (see Heb. 10:24–25). Esther was not foolish enough or so proud that she thought she could do this on her own; she knew she needed God's help and also the support of her people.

Note: It is interesting to read about Esther in the Apocrypha. It is well worth studying as it shows far more of Mordecai and Esther's personal faith in God, and includes a warning dream of Mordecai and their actual prayers for God's deliverance.

Week 5: Anger and Pride

Icebreaker

It may be useful to have in mind a few stories from
TV, newspapers or magazines. Stories about situations
such as road rage, gang warfare or revenge in a broken
relationship will lead into a good discussion.

Aim of the Session

Discussion Starters 1 and 2 encourage exploration into
the root of Haman's problems; this is probably the root
of much of the world's problems, too – self-centredness.
The character faults we see in Haman, Zeresh, his friends
and Xerxes seem to stem from this. Haman's interest
was in his wealth, power and position and he looked to
people around him to feed these ambitions. He had an
ingrained prejudice which closed his mind to any sense
of impartiality; others were viewed as having no value,
based on them having different ethnic origins.

To explore personal prejudices and their consequences
would be a practical way of using this material, though
if groups are to be open and honest with each other it
requires skilled, wise and sensitive leading. This also
applies to looking at anger and resentment in ourselves.
It may be helpful to give some space for people to reflect
quietly if a group discussion would feel threatening.

It is important to consider the antidote to this rather than
get stuck in the gloom that such discussions can lead to.
The passage from Philippians is a good place to start as
we look to Jesus, our great role model. Romans 12:9–21
is another passage that is useful to keep in mind. In
examining passages such as this, it is helpful to consider
how we read them. It is possible to read them as sets of
rules and principles that are good and must be obeyed,
yet feel overwhelmed and guilt-ridden as we see how
we do not live up to them. Alternatively, it is possible to

read such passages as an invitation, though a challenging one. We are invited to a way of life that is better, more wholesome, brings greater personal peace and contentment and creates harmony in our communities. This then leads to a desire to follow such standards, rather than feel failure to meet a demand. I have my own preferred way of addressing this issue, and as a leader it might be good to reflect on your own preferred approach.

A number of incidents described in the Old Testament occurred at night-time (see Discussion Starter 5). These often included dreams, but sometimes other occurrences – see for example Genesis 15:12–16; 28:10–15; 32:22–32 and chapters 40 and 41; Daniel 2; see also Numbers 12:6. God sometimes needs to catch our attention when we have stopped the activities which can often crowd Him out. If God is present at all times and in all places, there is no reason why He might not be present and at work in our times of sleep.

Discussion Starter 6 deals with Mordecai's origin. When God promised to make Abram's descendants into a great nation, He said, 'I will bless those who bless you, and whoever curses you I will curse' (Gen. 12:2–3). There is no reason to suppose that Haman's wife and friends were aware of this, but it seems that they had some understanding of the seriousness of opposing one of God's chosen people.

Discussion Starter 8 encourages us to reflect on Esther's attitudes and skills. She did not rush; she showed trust and patience as she allowed the work to be done in God's time. God seems absent but He is present and at work.

Note: You might also find it helpful either to start or finish this study with some meditative worship using part of Philippians chapter 2 to centre your thoughts on Jesus.

Week 6: Consequences

Icebreaker

Considering the action-adventure genre of movies will stimulate thought about why fictional violent death is often seen as entertainment. Is it ever helpful or thought-provoking? Should Christians view such material? Hopefully, this will lead into reflection on the *real* human cost when people lose their lives in disasters and catastrophic circumstances. (As leader, you may decide to suggest a few appropriate films that you personally have heard of or viewed.)

Aim of the Session

This is a challenging study, as we read of the mass destruction of the enemies of the Jews. It appears that the Jews, under Mordecai's instructions, were given the opportunity for revenge; this goes against all we learn about how Christians should behave towards those considered to be their enemies. Even outside the Church, revenge is often viewed as unacceptable. However, we need to think carefully about what this passage is saying, and attempt to read it in the context in which it was written.

Firstly, we need to consider the meaning of the word translated 'avenge' in Esther 8:13. Joyce Baldwin draws attention to the different emphasis in the words avenge, vengeance and vindicate, the latter being commendable as it is about defending what is right, whereas the former are more about an emotional reaction. The verb which is translated 'avenge' in the NIV translation means to inflict just punishment rather than to take vengeance. This word is used many times in connection with God as He overcomes evil and brings about justice in the Old Testament.

Secondly, we need to remember that justice was much more direct in this period. This was the time of an eye for an eye (see Deut. 19:21).

Thirdly, there was an element of discipline in the Jews' actions. This was not about exacting revenge for personal grievances but about permission to fight for one day only, or two in the case of Susa – and this was rather than be slaughtered themselves. This prevented an ongoing vendetta.

An interesting element of restraint is shown as we read three times that no plunder was taken, despite the allowance made for it. It was a matter of course that a victorious army would plunder the resources of those they had beaten in war. Not to do so showed an unusual sense of self-control; the decision not to become rich at the expense of their enemies would have been noteworthy.

The Jews attacked only those who were clearly their enemies and those who hated them. They were given full permission to include the women and children but the account only mentions the men. This may indicate, though not with certainty, that the women and children were spared.

It should be remembered that if the Jews had not been given this concession to attack then many, many more lives would have been lost as the entire Jewish population in the Persian Empire could have been decimated.

Parts of the Old Testament will always prove challenging to our understanding of God. I offer the following comments to you as a suggestion for your thought and discussion in understanding this. The history of the Jewish people was one in which they had needed to wipe out their enemies in order to keep their religion pure because their religion depended on a *national* relationship with God, rather than a personal one – religious purity was necessary to survive as a nation. The coming of Jesus was to bring in a new age where people had the opportunity to have a personal relationship with God through His Son. The importance now is to keep that personal relationship pure rather than the national religion.

Discussion Starter 4: Note that when Constantine became Roman Emperor in the fourth century, people flocked to join the Church, which had previously suffered persecution.

Discussion Starter 7 will inevitably raise questions about the avenging principle, and as leader you may like to raise issues such as the Holocaust, Pol Pot's killing fields, the Tutsi massacre and so on.

Giving the opportunity for people to question and have open discussion is important in this study, along with a humility in recognising that our earthly minds may struggle at times to understand the ways of God.

Week 7: Celebrate with Joy!

Icebreaker
You will need some sheets of paper and pens for this Icebreaker. It will be a fun way to introduce the theme of joy and thanksgiving.

Aim of the Session
This study covers three main areas. One is to review and reflect on the characters. Different things will strike different people. It may be useful to have some large sheets of paper (old wallpaper will do) and encourage everyone to contribute their thoughts as they write their ideas up as a thought-shower. You may want to take a separate sheet for individual characters, or use different coloured pens for each of them.

The second area is that of remembering and celebrating. If you are leading a group study, why not add an eighth session to do something, such as have a meal together, as a celebration?

The third area, as suggested in Discussion Starter 6, is to consider the theology behind the story, which is an important element of studying Esther. It is important to leave enough time to explore this idea.

In her scholarly work on Esther,[3] Joyce Baldwin helpfully points out two aspects of theology that are central to this book. Firstly, we see two conflicting world-views. On the one hand, Haman believes in chance and fate and that he can engineer events in order to control history. He thinks he can annihilate God's people should he choose. On the other hand, we have Mordecai, who is assured that the world's history is not dependent on chance, nor on the powerful Haman, but that there is One who is above all, who is in control and is ready to bring 'relief and deliverance' (Esth. 4:14). Esther also recognises this. Secondly, Joyce Baldwin points out the stress on human initiative. Esther realises that she must do her duty and appeal to the king because human responsibility is important, but she also recognises that it is God who is ultimately responsible.

God is not just interested in bringing people to positions of spiritual authority and ministry; He is just as involved in raising some people to places of power and influence. Both sacred and secular are of importance to God. These theological positions underpin this narrative and so need to be acknowledged.

[1]Joyce Baldwin, *Tyndale Old Testament Commentaries* (Leicester: IVP, 2003) p63.

[2]Richard Foster, *Celebration of Discipline* (London: Hodder & Stoughton, 1991).

[3]Joyce Baldwin, *Esther – Tyndale Old Testament Commentary* (Leicester: IVP, 2003).

Be inspired by God.
Every day.

One-year subscriptions available for all titles

Cover to Cover Every Day

In-depth study of the Bible, book by book. Part of a five-year series. Available as an email subscription or on eBook and Kindle.

Every Day with Jesus

The popular daily Bible reading notes by Selwyn Hughes.

Inspiring Women Every Day

Daily insight and encouragement written by women for women.

Life Every Day

Lively Bible notes, with Jeff Lucas' wit and wisdom.

To order or subscribe, visit **www.cwr.org.uk/store** or call **01252 784700**.
Also available in Christian bookshops.

 Print subscription available

 **Large Print subscription available**

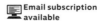 **Email subscription available**

Latest Resources

The Popular *Cover to Cover* Bible Study Series

1 Corinthians
Growing a Spirit-filled church
ISBN: 978-1-85345-374-8

2 Corinthians
Restoring harmony
ISBN: 978-1-85345-551-3

1 Peter
Good reasons for hope
ISBN: 978-1-78259-088-0

2 Peter
Living in the light of God's promises
ISBN: 978-1-78259-403-1

1 Timothy
*Healthy churches –
effective Christians*
ISBN: 978-1-85345-291-8

23rd Psalm
The Lord is my shepherd
ISBN: 978-1-85345-449-3

2 Timothy and Titus
Vital Christianity
ISBN: 978-1-85345-338-0

Abraham
Adventures of faith
ISBN: 978-1-78259-089-7

Acts 1-12
Church on the move
ISBN: 978-1-85345-574-2

Acts 13-28
To the ends of the earth
ISBN: 978-1-85345-592-6

Barnabas
Son of encouragement
ISBN: 978-1-85345-911-5

Bible Genres
Hearing what the Bible really says
ISBN: 978-1-85345-987-0

Daniel
Living boldly for God
ISBN: 978-1-85345-986-3

David
A man after God's own heart
ISBN: 978-1-78259-444-4

Ecclesiastes
*Hard questions and
spiritual answers*
ISBN: 978-1-85345-371-7

Elijah
A man and his God
ISBN: 978-1-85345-575-9

Elisha
A lesson in faithfulness
ISBN: 978-1-78259-494-9

Ephesians
Claiming your inheritance
ISBN: 978-1-85345-229-1

Esther
For such a time as this
ISBN: 978-1-85345-511-7

Fruit of the Spirit
Growing more like Jesus
ISBN: 978-1-85345-375-5

Galatians
Freedom in Christ
ISBN: 978-1-85345-648-0

God's Rescue Plan
*Finding God's fingerprints
on human history*
ISBN: 978-1-85345-294-9

Great Prayers of the Bible
Applying them to our lives today
ISBN: 978-1-85345-253-6

Haggai
Motivating God's people
ISBN: 978-1-78259-686-8

Hebrews
Jesus – simply the best
ISBN: 978-1-85345-337-3

Hosea
The love that never fails
ISBN: 978-1-85345-290-1

Isaiah 1-39
Prophet to the nations
ISBN: 978-1-85345-510-0

Isaiah 40-66
Prophet of restoration
ISBN: 978-1-85345-550-6

Jacob
Taking hold of God's blessing
ISBN: 978-1-78259-685-1

James
Faith in action
ISBN: 978-1-85345-293-2

Jeremiah
The passionate prophet
ISBN: 978-1-85345-372-4

John's Gospel
Exploring the seven miraculous signs
ISBN: 978-1-85345-295-6

Joseph
The power of forgiveness and reconciliation
ISBN: 978-1-85345-252-9

Joshua 1-10
Hand in hand with God
ISBN: 978-1-85345-542-7

Judges 1-8
The spiral of faith
ISBN: 978-1-85345-681-7

Judges 9-21
Learning to live God's way
ISBN: 978-1-85345-910-8

Luke
A prescription for living
ISBN: 978-1-78259-270-9

Mark
Life as it is meant to be lived
ISBN: 978-1-85345-233-8

Mary
The mother of Jesus
ISBN: 978-1-78259-402-4

Moses
Face to face with God
ISBN: 978-1-85345-336-6

Names of God
Exploring the depths of God's character
ISBN: 978-1-85345-680-0

Nehemiah
Principles for life
ISBN: 978-1-85345-335-9

Parables
Communicating God on earth
ISBN: 978-1-85345-340-3

Philemon
From slavery to freedom
ISBN: 978-1-85345-453-0

Philippians
Living for the sake of the gospel
ISBN: 978-1-85345-421-9

Prayers of Jesus
Hearing His heartbeat
ISBN: 978-1-85345-647-3

Proverbs
Living a life of wisdom
ISBN: 978-1-85345-373-1

Revelation 1-3
Christ's call to the Church
ISBN: 978-1-85345-461-5

Revelation 4-22
The Lamb wins! Christ's final victory
ISBN: 978-1-85345-411-0

Rivers of Justice
Responding to God's call to righteousness today
ISBN: 978-1-85345-339-7

Ruth
Loving kindness in action
ISBN: 978-1-85345-231-4

The Armour of God
Living in His strength
ISBN: 978-1-78259-583-0

The Beatitudes
Immersed in the grace of Christ
ISBN: 978-1-78259-495-6

The Covenants
God's promises and their relevance today
ISBN: 978-1-85345-255-0

The Creed
Belief in action
SBN: 978-1-78259-202-0

The Divine Blueprint
God's extraordinary power in ordinary lives
ISBN: 978-1-85345-292-5

The Holy Spirit
Understanding and experiencing Him
ISBN: 978-1-85345-254-3

The Image of God
His attributes and character
ISBN: 978-1-85345-228-4

The Kingdom
Studies from Matthew's Gospel
ISBN: 978-1-85345-251-2

The Letter to the Colossians
In Christ alone
ISBN: 978-1-855345-405-9

The Letter to the Romans
Good news for everyone
ISBN: 978-1-85345-250-5

The Lord's Prayer
Praying Jesus' way
ISBN: 978-1-85345-460-8

The Prodigal Son
Amazing grace
ISBN: 978-1-85345-412-7

The Second Coming
Living in the light of Jesus' return
ISBN: 978-1-85345-422-6

The Sermon on the Mount
Life within the new covenant
ISBN: 978-1-85345-370-0

Thessalonians
Building Church in changing times
ISBN: 978-1-78259-443-7

The Ten Commandments
Living God's Way
ISBN: 978-1-85345-593-3

The Uniqueness of our Faith
What makes Christianity distinctive?
ISBN: 978-1-85345-232-1

For current prices or to order, visit **www.cwr.org.uk/store**
Available online or from Christian bookshops.

SmallGroup central

All of our small group ideas and resources in one place

Online:

www.smallgroupcentral.org.uk
is filled with free video teaching,
tools, articles and a whole host
of ideas.

On the road:

A range of seminars themed for
small groups can be brought to
your local community. Contact us at
hello@smallgroupcentral.org.uk

In print:

Books, study guides and DVDs
covering an extensive list of themes,
Bible books and life issues.

Log on and find out more at:
www.smallgroupcentral.org.uk

Courses and events

Waverley Abbey College

Publishing and media

Conference facilities

Transforming lives

CWR's vision is to enable people to experience personal transformation through applying God's Word to their lives and relationships.

Our Bible-based training and resources help people around the world to:
• Grow in their walk with God
• Understand and apply Scripture to their lives
• Resource themselves and their church
• Develop pastoral care and counselling skills
• Train for leadership
• Strengthen relationships, marriage and family life and much more.

Our insightful writers provide daily Bible reading notes and other resources for all ages, and our experienced course designers and presenters have gained an international reputation for excellence and effectiveness.

CWR's Training and Conference Centres in Surrey and East Sussex, England, provide excellent facilities in idyllic settings – ideal for both learning and spiritual refreshment.

CWR Applying God's Word
to everyday life and relationships

CWR, Waverley Abbey House,
Waverley Lane, Farnham,
Surrey GU9 8EP, UK

Telephone: **+44 (0)1252 784700**
Email: **info@cwr.org.uk**
Website: **www.cwr.org.uk**

Registered Charity No. 294387
Company Registration No. 1990308